DREAMS, DOORS, AND DEGREES

2000-2001 NWMS READING BOOKS

RESOURCE BOOK FOR THE LEADER

CELEBRATE THE HARVEST
Edited by J. Wesley Eby

FOR THE READER

DREAMS, DOORS, AND DEGREES
The Story of Africa Nazarene University
By Theodore P. Esselstyn

IS THAT YOU, GOD?
Responses to the Mission Call
By Pat Stockett Johnston

THE MIRACLE GOES ON
European Nazarene Bible College
By Connie Griffith Patrick

THE MOUNTAIN KINGDOM
Claiming Lesotho for Christ
By Pat Stotler

TO SEE, TO BUILD, TO WIN
Volunteers for the Kingdom
By Carol Anne Eby

VENTURE OF THE HEART
Nazarene Missions in Peru
By Lela Morgan

DREAMS DOORS AND DEGREES

THE STORY OF AFRICA NAZARENE UNIVERSITY

Theodore P. Esselstyn

Nazarene Publishing House
Kansas City, Missouri

Copyright 2000
by Nazarene Publishing House

ISBN 083-411-8602

Printed in the
United States of America

Editor: J. Wesley Eby

Cover design: Kevin Williamson

10   9   8   7   6   5   4   3   2   1

CONTENTS

Theodore P. Esselstyn and his wife, Joan, have been Nazarene missionaries in Africa since 1968. Theodore, better known as Ted, is the son of William and Margaret Esselstyn, who were missionaries in Africa. Ted's missionary service of more than three decades has been in the field of education. Since 1983 he has been the education coordinator of the entire Africa Region.

FOREWORD

Africa. The sound of the word—once synonymous with adventure, beauty, and unsurpassed wildlife that spawned exotic dreams and motivated Westerners to explore and discover its unending mysteries—has become a trumpet call for suffering and disarray. There are countless reasons to despair for Africa. At the end of the 1980s, per capita income was lower than it was 30 years earlier. Seventy percent of the world's poorest nations are in Africa. The region is slipping out of the third world into its own bleak category: the nth world.

Where does the Church of Jesus Christ feature in all of this? Early missionaries, compelled by Matthew 28:18-20 and driven by their love for Christ and the people of His world, followed in the wake of the early explorers. They braved the perils of long sea voyages and hazardous overland journeys to stake out their claims with only frugal means at their disposal. Clinging to the promises and admonitions of God's Word, they began to bandage wounds, take care of sick bodies, and open schools and classrooms. As the church expanded, a victorious growing army of Christ's soldiers commenced proclaiming the start of a new era. Ethical principles, based on God's Word, liberated the people of this continent from the fear and bondage of witchcraft and heathen tradition. The word of the Lord to "love the Lord your God with all your heart and with all your soul and with all your mind" and "to love your neighbor as yourself" (Matthew 22:37, 39) became the supreme commandment.

The Church of the Nazarene is still on the march. Soon after I started my current assignment as director of the Africa Region in 1980, I recognized that equipping young and nurturing seasoned saints within our Zion could not be confined to the heart. I found only one ordained Nazarene elder with a university degree in all of Black Africa. Initially, we sent prospective university candidates overseas. Apart from the expense, the separation of husband and wife, of father and children, for an extended period proved heavy and often ended in a damaged or even a destroyed marital relationship. Added to that was an inability and sometimes unwillingness to readjust to African lifestyle.

I dreamed and asked the question, *A university in Africa—why not?* I presented the thought to my field directors and coleaders. It took 11 long years. It took courage to trust God. We had to step into the waters of the Jordan. And today we have the reality. Oh yes, there is still a long way to go. But a beginning has been made. We are on the road to victory.

—Richard F. Zanner, Africa Region director

ACKNOWLEDGMENTS

I acknowledge the significant contributions of Dr. Mark Moore, Dr. Harmon Schmelzenbach, and Dr. Leah Marangu in providing materials for incorporation into this book.

I am grateful for the invaluable assistance of Wes Eby in editing this book.

I appreciate the many ANU students who took time to write their concepts of the university, many of which are included in this book.

With thanks,

Theodore P. Esselstyn

PREFACE

Nazarene Education in Africa

Harambee—"working together." This Swahili word best expresses the miracle that has taken place on the outskirts of Nairobi. Nothing would have happened without the joint efforts of Nazarenes and the miracles that have flowed from the hand of God. *Harambee** made a dream—a dream in the hearts of African Nazarenes and their missionaries—become a reality. Even the writing of this record has taken the joint efforts of the author and his colleagues, Harmon Schmelzenbach and Mark Moore. Nevertheless, the miracle rising from the plains of Masai land just west of Nairobi is the work of one Person—the Person of our Lord. He gave the dream. He opened the door. He did the planning. He brought it into being.

African tradition placed education in the hands of tribal leadership. Missionaries saw education as a door to the gospel. Colonial governments saw education a responsibility of the state and in time took control of education. In countries like South Africa, the state physically took over mission schools, making them government institutions. The focus was on training, not on the education of leadership. An elitist system allowed only the privileged few to re-

*A pronunciation guide is provided on pages 95-96 for words that may be unfamiliar to the reader.

ceive leadership education. The colonial system was the education pattern inherited by the nations of Africa as they became independent.

Education is still controversial in Africa. Many of the governments are reworking their systems with vigor and courage. Among them is the country of Kenya. This nation made an assessment of its education system and initiated a radical change, calling for continuing assessment of outcomes and needed revision to meet current needs. The government leaders aim to produce leaders, creative entrepreneurs, qualified educators, and gifted managers, who can bring strength to every facet of the economy and country. For the first time, the door opened for non-government organizations to establish institutions in Africa similar to Christian colleges and universities in America.

The Church of the Nazarene has always been involved in education. Denominational leaders have known how important it is for young people to have a sound understanding of the world and of the Word. In Africa, wherever the church took root, primary schools, high schools, and theological colleges were started. In Swaziland, Nazarene missionaries started the first nursing college, the first teacher training college, several high schools, and a multitude of primary schools. They helped to write curriculum for all schools. The government showed thanks with grants of money and salaries for the teachers and administrators.

Unfortunately, with time, control passed to the Swaziland Education Department. In South Africa, the Church of the Nazarene had a nursing college along with many primary and high schools, but all were taken over by the government. In Mozambique, there were severe limitations on education. Since graduates of high school became citizens, the state insisted on total control of the high schools. Nazarenes were only allowed to operate a primary school and, under its auspices, a Bible college.

Church organizations could open Bible and theological colleges throughout most of Africa. In 1980 the Church of the Nazarene had nine Bible colleges in southern Africa alone. Since then, the church has refined and strengthened its theological schools. Where possible, the church merged institutions, opened colleges as new countries were entered, and established extension systems to train pastors unable to attend college. But, until Kenya changed its system, the door had been firmly shut to the provision of quality holiness higher education for the youth of the church.

Africa Nazarene University is the reality that God is providing to fulfill the dreams of His people.

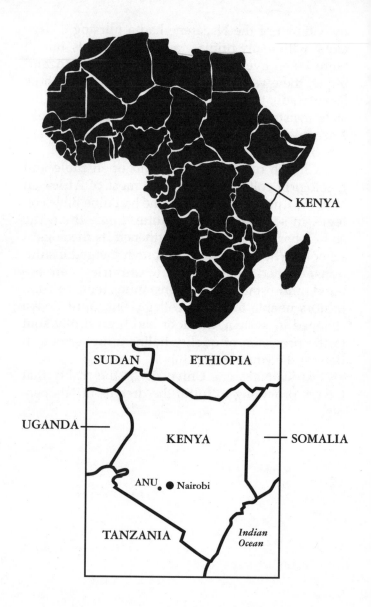

KENYA

SUDAN
ETHIOPIA
UGANDA
KENYA
SOMALIA
ANU ● Nairobi
TANZANIA
Indian
Ocean

CHAPTER 1

DREAMING

Theodore Esselstyn was born and raised on the mission field in Africa. During his youth, Ted, as most people know him, visited many countries of Africa with his parents. While visiting Malawi, God showed him that hope for the transformation of Africa lay with African pastors and laypeople. The next 13 years Ted spent at college, seminary, and graduate school in the United States, preparing to train church leaders. During those years, he met Joan Kehm, they married, and the couple had three children.

Joan and Ted went to Africa as Nazarene missionaries in 1968, at a time when no Black pastor in the Church of the Nazarene in Africa had finished high school. The Esselstyns first served at Lula Schmelzenbach Memorial Nazarene Bible College at Arthurseat, in the warm lowvelt of South Africa with myriad snakes and mosquitoes, with roaming antelope and lions. Among the teachers were Samson Mkabela, who had taken his Bible training under Ted's father, William Esselstyn, at the first Nazarene school at Pigg's Peak. Another was Enoch Litswele, a graduate of Swaziland Nazarene Bible College. Enoch had served at the Malawi Bible College and opened the first Nazarene church in Harare, Zimbabwe.

Together with Paul Dayhoff, the principal and a missionary, the men often talked and dreamed of the future. At times the first African district superintendent, Enos Mokwena, a powerful holiness leader and preacher, joined the group. Samson raised a question that came to haunt Ted: "When will my children be able to go to a Nazarene university?" The church did not have a degree program anywhere on the continent. Although the first step was soon taken to set up a theological degree course, a Nazarene university remained in the realm of dreams.

Missionary leaders joined forces with the then Home Missions Department, which had established Nazarene Bible College of South Africa. Missionary Floyd Perkins, the principal, had established links with Canadian Nazarene College. By 1973, the bachelor of theology degree was offered on several campuses. Five years later, the first Black graduate joined the pastoral team in southern Africa, thanks to Canadian Nazarene College. Today, more than a score of graduates have earned master's degrees, and a few have gone on to doctoral work. But this did not fulfill the dream of a holiness university.

> *"Nazarenes believe education and*
> *evangelism are Siamese twins*
> *in the ministry of holiness."*

By 1980, the Church of the Nazarene was in eight African countries: Cape Verde, Malawi, Mozambique, Namibia, South Africa, Swaziland, Zambia, and Zimbabwe. But, the laws in these lands provided only for government-controlled degrees. Church leaders were frustrated, for they believed what General Superintendent John Knight said so well at the 1997 General Assembly, "Nazarenes believe education and evangelism are Siamese twins in the ministry of holiness."

The second step to quality education came from the staff of the Ethel Lucas Memorial Hospital before it was taken over by the South African government. They established a bursary (scholarship) fund to help Bible college students and pastors' children obtain a higher education. This was the first scholarship endowment. By 1984 all Nazarene colleges united their scholarship funds into an investment program. Since then, this endowment has grown, providing funds that have opened the door of opportunity for more than 2,100 Nazarene youth.

But nonministerial education or graduate study in a holiness environment was only possible if students could go to America. The economies of Africa and the United States are so vastly different that this is seldom possible. When it is, the "good life" lures many to stay in America. The cost prevents most married students from taking their spouses, which sometimes has resulted in the breakup of the family. The development of scholarship funds was not enough—the Church of the Nazarene needed an institution for holiness higher education in Africa.

The year 1980 was one of transition for Africa

when the regional structure of the Church of the Nazarene was born. The Africa Field came into existence 70 years before. Much later in 1959, church leaders divided the continent into five regions coordinated by a common executive committee. By 1971 growth reached the point that church leaders made each region a field on its own and abolished the executive committee. Fields soon lost touch with each other, becoming quite independent. An unexpected result was that no field felt responsibility to enter new countries. Outreach stopped. The vision for the rest of Africa seemed to die.

Then Richard Zanner, superintendent of the Middle European District, was appointed to unite Africa into one region as its first director. God used Dr. Zanner to unite the fragmented fields and give them an evangelistic concern for all of Africa.

Expansion in the 20 years since then has been stunning: Angola, Botswana, Congo, Côte d'Ivoire, Democratic Republic of Congo, Eritrea, Ethiopia, Ghana, Kenya, Lesotho, Liberia, Madagascar, Nigeria, Senegal, Rwanda, Tanzania, and Uganda. The national church has, in New Testament style, entered into Benin, Burkina Faso, Burundi, Cameroon, Djibouti, Gabon, Sao Tomé and Principe, Somalia, Sudan, and Togo.

More than 200,000 Nazarenes now live on the African continent. The growth rate is frightening to those involved in preparing ministers. The current demand across the region is for more than 200 new pastors each year. Nazarene theological schools need to have 800 full-time students just to meet that need.

The success of evangelism and the use of the *JESUS* film threaten to more than triple even this need.

"Leaders, O Lord, give us leaders" was—and still is—the cry to heaven. Dr. Zanner's initial dream was frustrated by the shortage of leadership. He was stunned to find that not even five ordained African pastors had finished high school in 1980. The new degree program was just beginning to produce fruit. Drastic steps needed to be taken.

Dr. Zanner appointed Ted Esselstyn as education coordinator for the Africa Region in 1983. Ted was charged with the responsibility to help the colleges work together, upgrade the education program, and concentrate on preparing quality ministers. The need for graduate education for ministers was recognized, and consideration was given to starting a seminary-level institution in Africa. Yet, the laws of the lands where the church was well-established would not permit church-controlled degree-granting institutions. South Africa, which had the best Nazarene and commercial infrastructure, at this time was totally unacceptable to the rest of Africa.

Most of West Africa, other than Ghana, Liberia, and Nigeria, is French-speaking. Dr. Zanner invited John and Linda Seaman, serving in Martinique, to open this field. They settled in Abidjan, Côte d'Ivoire. This move incorporated the church in Nigeria that had long tried to become a part of the denomination. They needed a Bible college to provide training for the 80 or more lay pastors who were caring for the churches. Today, the church operates education programs at multiple centers in Benin, Cape Verde, Côte d'Ivoire, Ghana, Liberia, Nigeria, and Senegal. But none of these countries gave the church the opportunity to establish a holiness higher-education institution.

For some years Kenyans, who had attended Nazarene colleges in the United States and had joined the church, called for Nazarenes to come to their country. God moved Dr. Zanner to visit Kenya, and he was convinced that the time had come to enter Kenya. In 1984 he approached veteran missionaries Harmon and Beverly Schmelzenbach, serving in Namibia. He challenged them to open a new field in East Africa, starting in the city of Nairobi.

God had prepared the Schmelzenbachs for this task. Harmon traversed Kenya in packed *matatus* along with the Kenyans. This mode of transportation provided opportunity to talk to people and learn about their culture and land. Harmon was inundated with requests to "come and preach in my town." The desire to join the Church of the Nazarene grew, particularly after Kenyans learned that the church established strong educational institutions. Kenyans wanted quality education, and a new door was about to swing open for the church.

CHAPTER 2

BEGINNING IN KENYA

Harmon Schmelzenbach stood to speak at Angel Stadium in Anaheim, California, on a hot Sunday afternoon of the 1985 General Assembly. He had in his hand nearly three dozen handwritten applications to the ministry of the Church of the Nazarene. They came from Kenyans wanting to become a part of a Holiness church in East Africa.

Harmon and Beverly had been in Kenya for only six months. During that time, he had preached in dozens of marketplaces. He was swamped with inquiries from young people, saying: "I feel God is calling me to the ministry. Do you have a Bible school?" and "How can I enroll?"

Harmon concluded his report to the thousands of Nazarenes in the baseball stadium with these words: "What do I do with these letters? How do I train them? Beverly and I are alone in East Africa!"

No one could have anticipated the response. In the next few years, through a relatively new church program called Work and Witness, more than a thousand Nazarenes flew to Kenya to help in the building of the Kingdom. For Africa Nazarenes, they became a legion of angels.

In the meantime, Harmon followed his grandfather's example. He copied the old quarterly meetings that lasted several days every three months. During that time, he taught pastors what he could to improve their ministry and inspire their hearts. He also discussed the practical and personal problems each one faced. This plan had worked in Swaziland with pioneer missionary Harmon F. Schmelzenbach, for out of it grew the great church that exists in Africa today.

Harmon contacted Ted Esselstyn, and together they planned a two-week training and indoctrination course called an Intensive. Ted brought teachers; Harmon promised students. Ted was skeptical that there could be 10 prospective ministerial students after just six months. Harmon wrote to 70 selected men from the many applications and invited them to come to Nairobi for 10 days. There were no strings attached, for the men did not know the church and the church did not know them. This would be a time of becoming acquainted as well as training.

To walk into a hall and find it packed with more than a hundred eager and vocal young preachers was exciting.

Lodrick Gama, a teacher at Swaziland Nazarene Bible College, helped with the teaching. Leo Mpoke, a Kenyan with an American educational background who worked in Nazarene Compassionate Ministries, taught a course in recordkeeping and finance. Rowena Gastineau, who with her husband had just arrived as missionaries in Kenya, taught women's ministries and a Sunday School course. At the first Intensive, 27 prospective pastors attended. God's presence was overwhelming; the excitement was electric. Plans were laid for a system of Intensives running from two to three weeks every six months. Each one got bigger, until at maximum capacity about 120 students attended. The limiting factors were budget and facilities, not applicants.

By the third and fourth Intensives, the program had a life of its own. To walk into a hall and find it packed with more than a hundred eager and vocal young preachers was exciting. It really does something to see this many men, eager to serve God and already on fire. Many of them had finished high school and spoke good English. Their cry was for education—good theological training.

During the next years, Nazarenes from many parts of the world were involved in the program. Dr. William Prince came from the European Nazarene Bible College, where he was serving as rector. Dr. Steven Manley, Nazarene evangelist, gave time to teach evangelism and to preach each evening. Their ministry was challenging, and they gave of themselves freely to the students. Years later, Dr. Prince saw some of the fruits of his labor when he returned as general superintendent to ordain men whom he had taught.

One person sent ripples right across the new work, since a strong bias existed in Kenya against women in the preaching ministry. Rev. Juliet Ndzimandze, one of the most outstanding Swazi preachers, came to minister. Her preaching, along with her great love for God and all people, won the hearts of the students. Rev. Ndzimandze served as a catalyst to help the African church recognize the place of women in the pulpit.

God was establishing the church in East Africa. Congregations began to spring up. Central Church of the Nazarene started to grow in the house Harmon and Bev had procured in Nairobi, and it continued to grow. Among the charter members were John and Leah Marangu, graduates of Olivet Nazarene University, who had gone on to earn Ph.D. degrees in the United States. They had returned to take positions at Kenyatta University, where both were full professors and heads of departments.

Little known to the many involved, God was about to open the door for the fulfillment of the dream to provide quality holiness education for the youth of the Church of the Nazarene in Africa.

CHAPTER 3

ENTERING THE OPEN DOOR

During one of the early Intensives, an event took place that was to have a profound effect upon the Africa Region. A scandal hit the papers regarding a schemer who tried to make his fortune by opening a bogus private university. This caught people's attention. The remarkable fact was that the papers indicated a private university was possible in Kenya. This was a radical departure from the educational pattern in the rest of Africa.

Harmon and Ted went to John and Leah Marangu to find out the meaning of these statements and learned that the government of Kenya had changed the educational system. A Commission for Higher Education had been created and given jurisdiction to accredit and charter private universities. John, in his quiet manner, proudly stated, "Leah is one of the commissioners." The more they talked, the more it became obvious that the long sought education door was being opened in Kenya.

Harmon began to investigate the possibility, which led him to the office of the Ministry of Education, Science, and Technology. In 1986, he was advised to contact the secretary of the Commission for

Higher Education. John Marangu, Harmon Schmelzenbach, and Ted Esselstyn made an appointment to meet Dr. Joseph Mungai, an eminent Kenyan surgeon and professor, who was the head of the Commission's secretariat and a former vice-chancellor of Nairobi University.

A seminary for ministerial training was a most urgent need.

Although the Church of the Nazarene in Africa had few ordained men and women with a degree at this time, there were Nazarene medical doctors, lawyers, and businessmen. There were politicians who had risen to high positions in their governments. But there were only a few ministers who had the ability and training to conserve such a harvest. Ted had prepared to try to address this shortcoming. The new educational opportunities in Kenya and the need for a Bible college for East Africa combined to indicate that Kenya might be the place where the dream for a Nazarene college in Africa could be fulfilled. A seminary for ministerial training was a most urgent need. After discussing this with Richard Zanner, Ted made the formal proposal at the Regional Advisory Committee meeting in Johannesburg that a graduate school for ministerial training be established. A proposal was drafted to the Board of General Superintendents for the establishment of a graduate-level school called Africa Nazarene Seminary to be located in Nairobi, Kenya.

Dr. Charles Strickland, former missionary to Africa, was the general superintendent in jurisdiction in Africa at that time. After presenting the proposal to the Board of General Superintendents, he wrote "I received a favorable vote from the Board to recommend to World Mission the building of a graduate-level school in Kenya with some future consideration of a seminary."

The 1985 General Assembly established an education commission to study Nazarene education around the world. This set the stage for the Kenya venture. Gifts were already coming in for the Kenya college. Church leaders were able to begin the long process of negotiation with the Commission for Higher Education in Kenya to start a degree-granting institution. The commission considered any school that granted degrees in any discipline as a university. Furthermore, it strongly suggested that the church open a liberal arts institution.

By February 1987 the Kenya District had 70 active preaching points, each of which could become an organized church. The shortage of workers was the block to development of churches and districts. Even though 12 Kenyan students enrolled at Swaziland Nazarene Bible College (2,000 miles from Kenya) in 1986 and 7 more in 1987, there was no way to maintain this expense. The Church of the Nazarene had to start a degree-level school.

The need existed, and God was working. It was time to enter the open door.

CHAPTER 4

FOLLOWING GOD'S PLAN

Some Christians believe God only works at the last minute. The Bible, however, shows that God plans far ahead. He even says that He planned for Jesus the Lamb to take away our sin before He made the world! Certainly God planned years ahead for Africa Nazarene University. He had been preparing many different people for various aspects of the task.

Harmon Schmelzenbach

One such person was Harmon Schmelzenbach. The grandson of the founder of the mission work of the Church of the Nazarene in Swaziland, Harmon grew up on the mission field in the home of his missionary parents, Elmer and Mary Schmelzenbach. A burden for evangelizing Africa was deep in his heart. God brought him back to Africa with Beverly and seasoned them in the rugged environment of Sekhukhuneland. He took them into Botswana, where Harmon registered the Church of the Nazarene. He challenged them with the new area of Namibia, a vast desert land. This was their preparation for the opening of the work of the Church of the Nazarene in East Africa.

Harmon Schmelzenbach

When the Schmelzenbachs arrived in Nairobi in 1983, they discovered God had prepared others. When the Commission for Higher Education granted the Letter of Interim Authority many years later, the vice-chancellor of one of the universities of Kenya said to Harmon, "I have been praying that you Nazarenes would be successful in this great venture." Thirty-five years earlier, while a student in the United States, this vice-chancellor had sat under the ministry of Dr. Eugene Stowe at College Church, Nampa, Idaho, for six years.

This reminded Harmon that years before God had brought together at Northwest Nazarene College (now University) (NNU) several people who would be involved in developing the university: he and Beverly; Al Jones, who was then NNU's student body president; and Bob Helstrom, a fellow student. Thirty-five years earlier the Master had started to move players into place for establishing a university deep inside Africa.

Richard Zanner

Richard Zanner

Another person God was preparing was Richard Zanner. Son of a military officer, Richard and his brothers found the mining community of South Africa to be the door of opportunity for German youth. Ambitious, brilliant, and energetic, Richard's fortunes rose. He met his wife, Valerie, daughter of charter members of the Horison Church of the Nazarene in Roodepoort, South Africa. Through Valerie's family, Dr. Charles Strickland came into Richard's life, and through Dr. Strickland, Jesus Christ.

*Richard, who dynamited mine shafts
to seek for gold in the bowels of Africa,
became a student of the Word, seeking
gold in the hearts of humankind.*

Richard, a master blaster, who dynamited mine shafts to seek for gold in the bowels of Africa, became a student of the Word, seeking gold in the hearts of humankind. Dr. Jerald Johnson, then a missionary in Europe, heard of this German in South Africa and called him to return to Germany, first to pastor and then to lead the district. God was preparing Richard to fill the role of regional director in the Church of the Nazarene. God gave him roots in Africa, a vision for the transformation of the continent, and an unusual ability to manage finance that was vital in the struggling economy of Africa—all keys to the establishment of the university.

Theodore Esselstyn

A third player in God's plans was Ted Esselstyn. He was the son of missionaries, William and Margaret Esselstyn, born while they served in Siteki, Swaziland. They had been on the field nine years and furlough was more than due, but God kept them in Swaziland until their last son arrived. Three months later, they furloughed, never to return to live in Swaziland, but rather to live near Johannesburg. Ted grew up in South Africa in the mining belt surrounding the metropolitan center.

When Ted was born in 1937, God knew what

Ted Esselstyn

the politics of the United States would be in the 1960s, and of Africa and the world in the 1980s. He had planned for it. Ted went to Eastern Nazarene College (ENC) in Wollaston, Massachusetts, and then on to Nazarene Theological Seminary in Kansas City. Finally God opened the door to Yale University in Connecticut. Ted had extremely limited funds. Since Yale offered a substantial scholarship, Dean Bertha Munro of ENC strongly encouraged him to accept. Later, Ted discovered that during the antidiscrimination days of the '60s, when no pictures were permitted on applications and progressive universities sought Black students, officials thought "born in Swaziland" meant Black. God had planned ahead.

Ted and Joan went to Africa in 1968—first to the Lula Schmelzenbach Memorial Nazarene Bible

College. It was here that Nazarene giants such as Enoch Litswele, Samson Mkabela, and Enos Mokwena were instrumental in instructing his thinking and awakening in his heart their vision for Africa's youth. Ted then went to the Nazarene Bible College of South Africa, where he became rector. This opened the door for him to lead the degree-level program for Nazarene ministers.

In 1983 Dr. Zanner conceived the idea of an education coordinator for the church in Africa. When he invited Ted to take this position, at first this appeared to be impossible as Ted was an American living in South Africa. Once again, God's planning was revealed. Until Ted was born, God had kept his parents in Swaziland, and his birth in Swaziland opened the door to the rest of Africa. Travel during the '80s was barred to any American who lived in or visited South Africa, but not to those born in a front-line state, and Swaziland was a front-line state. God had planned ahead.

Mark Reynolds Moore

A fourth person God prepared, Mark Moore, was a bundle of pure energy. He was well seasoned by the Lord—chaplain in World War II, prisoner in a German camp, pastor, district superintendent, president of Trevecca Nazarene University, and secretary of education for the Church of the Nazarene. In these roles he came to know the church and refined the arts of managing people, raising finances, and getting the job done.

When their phone rang in the fall of 1987, Mark

Mark and Clarice Moore

and Clarice were just beginning to enjoy retirement. They had settled into their own home for the first time in their lives. He was program director on a cruise ship for the Nazarene Celebration at Sea. And when his wife, Clarice, asked what the long call was about, he struggled to find the answer.

Mark thought, *How do I answer her? We have spent 50 years together in various assignments. We have always made decisions together. I must trust God and her to help me reach the proper decision.* Then he told his wife, "That was Dr. Esselstyn calling from South Africa."

"What did he want?"

"Ted wanted to know if we would consider going to Kenya to establish a graduate seminary and a university." Mark waited for Clarice's response.

After careful contemplation, she said, "Sounds like a real challenge. I think you could make a contribution." In that simple sentence, Clarice knew that if the plans developed, it meant giving up a home, security, retirement, and family. God had prepared a committed man and woman who were to make an indelible imprint upon the face of Africa.

Leah Marangu

One more person in God's planning must be considered—Leah Marangu. Her story is quite different. She grew up in a society where girls seldom went to school. The role of the woman was to care for the home and children. But she grew up under the influence of English Methodist missionaries who worked in Kenya. Her father, a prominent man in the community, sent her to primary school. He was progressive and felt that education, at least reading and writing, was necessary in the world in which his children would live. Leah proved to be an outstanding student. When primary school was complete, her mother insisted her daughter return home and develop those skills that would make her a successful Kenyan mother.

As with most girls of her culture, education appeared to end. But God was not ready for that. The

Lord moved Leah's teacher to inquire about her prize student. She packed her suitcase and walked many miles to the village where Leah lived. There she sat down with Leah's mother, finally convincing her that Leah should continue in school. Leah graduated at the top of her class.

Leah graduated at the top of her class.

Not far from her home lived a young man, John Marangu. Later, John and Leah were married. His father had some wealth and a keen interest in the success of his sons. John also went to Methodist schools and performed in an outstanding manner. Wanting a university education, John gathered information and found on the list of American

Leah Marangu

schools the name of Olivet Nazarene College (now University). He was impressed that the college put "Nazarene" into its name, the name of his Lord, as well as "Olivet," the name of one of the places favored by Jesus. When John applied, he was accepted. Arriving in Chicago in midwinter, without jacket or sweater, he had a chilling introduction to life in America. However, the warmth of friendship by students and faculty at Olivet soon wrapped around him.

John wanted Leah to share in the fellowship and friendship he discovered at Olivet and sent for her. Since she had the qualifications, she enrolled in Olivet too. There they joined the Church of the Nazarene. The Marangus continued their studies until both had acquired master's degrees and doctorates. In the years that followed, Leah acquired 10 years experience in American public schools and 8 years in universities.

When the time was right, the Marangus returned to Kenya to serve at Kenyatta University in Nairobi. John, with his degree in genetics, was soon head of the biology department. Leah became the first woman in Kenya to become a full professor and the first to become a department head. She was appointed director of the Kenyatta Foundation, which produced texts for Kenya, and made it a resounding success. She wrote numerous textbooks and gathered a lengthy list of honors and achievements.

It was the Marangus who called out for their church to come to Kenya. It was John and Leah who became charter members of the first Church of the Nazarene in Kenya, Nairobi Central. It was also John and Leah who provided guidance to Mark Moore in developing the proposal for the university. And it was Leah who, in January 1996, accepted the position of vice-chancellor* to provide leadership for Africa Nazarene University.

Truly, God plans ahead.

---

*Vice-chancellor is the usual title for the head of a university in British Commonwealth countries. The chancellor is usually a figurehead, often the king or president of the country.

CHAPTER 5

MAKING THE PROPOSAL

The first step for creating a university was to make a formal proposal, which proved to be a complicated task. To make a proposal necessitated setting out a realistic projection of finance, property and facilities, administration, curriculum, faculty, and students.

The proposal for ANU was the first one submitted to the Commission for Higher Education in Kenya and became a learning process for them and for the Church of the Nazarene. The proposal needed the approval of the Division of World Mission, the General Board, and the Board of General Superintendents. Concurrently, the church was in the process of hearing and acting upon the report of the Commission on Education set up at the 1985 General Assembly. As the church and Kenya structures matured, meeting the requirements was quite a challenge.

Purchasing the Land

Harmon Schmelzenbach took on the task of obtaining suitable property. The year 1987 found America in the grip of a major recession, and the budget was limited. Yet, land was extremely expensive. Numerous possible sites were investigated.

The Commission for Higher Education had specified that any university-level institution would need at least 50 acres for approval. Such parcels of land were not common in a society where land is subdivided to the sons with each generation. Sites near utilities and good roads were far too costly. When Harmon and Bev shared this burden with everyone on their mailing list, a miracle started to take place. Funds designated for the institution started to arrive at the World Mission Division in Kansas City.

God led Harmon to some land on the outskirts of Nairobi, a site 14 miles from the center of the city. To the east is Nairobi's skyline. In between is the Nairobi National Park with no fence. The 70-acre property, bordered by a deep canyon with a small river, was mostly grass and bush with a variety of animals. Later, an adjacent 30 acres of flat land were added. The last two miles of the road to the site were a formidable obstacle.

The purchase of the land was complicated. It involved the four owners of the four plots being purchased, the district government, and, since the church was technically registered as a foreign institution, the office of the president (Department of the Interior). The four owners, church lawyers, government lawyers, Harmon, interested parliament members, and government advisers spent two days around a table. Finally, the ruling was given in the school's favor. Officials paid for the land, received the deeds, handed the deeds to the government, and received a 99-year lease. Construction could begin.

Once again, God had planned ahead. Richard Roles, a friend of the Schmelzenbachs, called Harmon to say he had sent $100,000 to provide a start-up fund for the university. Richard could not have foreseen the enormous impact of this initial gift and his many subsequent donations. Coupled with Work and Witness, it became possible to start building.

Setting Up the Administration

Setting up the administration and development structure was the next major task. Since the first step was selecting a head for the institution, Mark Moore with his vast experience accepted this responsibility.

Mark and Clarice experienced what all missionaries do—a mad rush to get everything done in time, coupled with a lot of waiting. They began preparation in the fall of 1987: getting shots, obtaining passports, selling their house, buying equipment, holding deputation services, and studying Kenya's profile. With such thorough preparation, they adapted to Kenya with surprising speed. Mark soon could rival the best of the Kenyan drivers, weaving his way through the hectic traffic as if he had been born to it. The Moores did much the same in their relationships with the Kenyan people; their love overflowed whether to officialdom or the person in the street. They quickly accepted the challenges of a new culture, and the people loved them.

As part of the preparation, Mark made a quick trip to Nairobi in January 1988 with Don Jernigan, who had offered to donate his services as architect for the university. They met with missionaries Harmon Schmelzenbach, Ted Esselstyn, and Roger Gastineau, along with a local architect, to develop plans for the university's first phase to include seven single-story buildings.

In February of that year, the General Board gave formal approval for the Moores' assignment. Immediately, Mark recruited Work and Witness teams, faculty, and specialists to help. Dr. Eugene Stowe, then general superintendent who spoke at the missionary-sending service in June in Overland Park, Kansas, had all the parents of recently appointed missionaries stand. When he noticed Brad Moore standing, he asked, "Brad, who are you sending?"

"I'm sending my parents to Nairobi, Kenya."

Securing the Property

A dozen lions killed cattle on the athletic field.

Once settled in Nairobi, Mark learned that one of the first jobs was to fence the 20 acres where the first buildings were to be located. Animals were—and still are—a concern. In 1997 a dozen lions killed cattle on the athletic field of the university. Students walking the last two miles to campus in early morning or late evening often see hyenas and once in a while even a leopard. Carol Rotz, a teacher, had to walk the last half-mile one morning and was confronted by a troop of hyenas. She remembered that the whistle she had been given while missionary-in-residence at Northwest Nazarene College (now University) (NNU) was still in her purse. Digging it out, she blew with all her might. The hyenas took off. Thanks to NNU, whistles have become popular at ANU. The sight of wild game became so common that even Work and Witness volunteers did not stop work to view them.

Animals continue to be a problem. Hyenas circle the fence nightly with their weird cries, seeking garbage from the university. When food becomes scarce in the dry season, leopards get bold and jump the fence to claw the security dogs, a favorite food, out of their kennels. Several dogs were lost before a kennel was built that would keep out the leopards. Perhaps the most annoying animal has been the tall, placid giraffe. After the lone telephone wire was strung across two miles of grassland, it was discovered that giraffes seldom deigned to duck. They simply walked through, breaking the wire and ending telephone service. The problem was eventually solved when a heavy multiline cable was strung—too strong for giraffes to break.

Establishing the Board of Trust

The next major step was the establishment of a Board of Trust. Professor Joseph Mungai, secretary for the Commission for Higher Education, had indicated that a legal body, a trust, was necessary to make the proposal for the university. This was required to guarantee the autonomy of the university from the state and any other body. He further indicated it would be best to call the institution Africa Nazarene University (ANU) and to seek accreditation for it from the commission. ANU was the first new institution to seek a charter under the new legislation. Until the letter of authority was granted by the Commission for Higher Education, the word *proposed* would need to be used in connection with the name.

Early in February 1989, a planning committee met to set the direction for the university. Their proposal with a suggested "Deed of Trust" was sent to Dr. Jerald Johnson, general superintendent in jurisdiction. Instructions were faxed from the General Board meeting in February 1989 to proceed with the establishment of the Africa Nazarene University Trust with seven members. The first Board of Trust consisted of Richard Zanner, Ted Esselstyn, Harmon Schmelzenbach, John Marangu, Cornelius Muthuri, Jason Kimbui, and Mark Moore. Later, the Trust was enlarged to include the general superintendent in jurisdiction of Africa. A University Council, representative of all Africa fields, was established to approve academic and administrative policy.

The 1989 General Superintendents' "Quadrennial Address" included recognition of the proposed Africa Nazarene University as the latest prospect for Nazarene education. In this same General Assembly, responding to the work of the Education Commission established in 1985, a commissioner of education and an International Board of Education were established to promote and assist with the development of higher education in the Church of the Nazarene around the world. The trust was processed by the lawyers in Kenya and formally registered in the presence of General Superintendent Johnson in January 1990.

Preparing the Proposal

The next major step was the preparation of the proposal for the university. This complicated and lengthy document delineated all aspects of the university—objectives, governance, academics, resources, personnel, students, and so forth. The proposal needed to be in Kenyan terms. John Marangu, who knew Nazarene higher education and the requirements of the Commission for Higher Education, headed a subcommittee of eight Kenyan professors to draft curriculum. This resulted in the first successful draft of the proposal. The Commission for Higher Education read and commented upon the proposal, and the process was underway.

During the next three years, two revisions were prepared and submitted before the Letter of Interim Authority was granted to allow the recruitment of students. The first revision integrated the curriculum with the Nazarene concept of a liberal arts education. The second one aligned the whole proposal with the requirements of universities in the British Commonwealth and resulted in receiving the Letter of Interim Authority.

After four years of successful operation, the university then could apply for the formal charter. During this time, the document, no longer a proposal but a charter document, would need to be reevaluated, updated, and refined.

Starting the Buildings

An essential need for any institution is buildings and grounds. When Robert Scott, then director of the World Mission Division, presented to the General Board the request to establish ANU, he informed them that the project would not be eligible for World Evangelism Fund support. However, other programs of the general church, such as Nazarenes in Volunteer Service and Work and Witness, would be available. In God's amazing providence, these two new programs came into being in time to make the project possible. Also, the more traditional methods of Alabaster, missionary deputation offerings, and general church specials could be used.

Mark Moore, knowing that in the economy of heaven the prayers of the saints are a valuable commodity, set about moving people to pray. God, His people, and the church did not fail. Thousands of participants have made, and still are making, contributions to ANU through a variety of avenues.

CHAPTER 6

VOLUNTEERING AND GIVING

African nationals and missionaries—along with Work and Witness teams, Nazarenes in Volunteer Service (NIVS), generous donors, and volunteers from around the world—have all been a part of the great team to bring ANU into existence. Unfortunately, there is insufficient space in this book to name and discuss all of them. But Africans will be forever thankful for the generosity of these people of God.

Work and Witness

David Hayse, then director of Work and Witness, after visiting Kenya in 1988, presented the challenge of ANU to prospective teams. Missionaries Roger and Rowena Gastineau set up an outstanding program to host the teams. Each group had opportunity to meet the church in Kenya, work on university buildings, and sample the wildlife for which Kenya is famous. Exotic meals and market visits helped enrich the African experience. Marion Miller served as the project supervisor for the buildings, uniting the efforts of the teams into a coherent result. Don Jernigan, working with a local architect, provided the plans.

Rev. Hayse appointed Bob and Yvonne Helstrom as ANU's Work and Witness coordinators. A toll-free phone line, a booth at the General Assembly, a page on the Internet, and support for NIVS have been part of the Helstroms' generous contributions. During the years that Mark Moore served at ANU, 50 teams, averaging 16 people each, went to Kenya and contributed more than $500,000 in cash.

Work and Witness remains one of the major forces in the plans for the university.

Team members laid Kenyan hand-cut stones for walls, set clay tiles on the roof, made steel rafters, windows, and doorframes, and put in electric service and plumbing. Kenyan laborers helped with digging foundations, mixing and pouring concrete, and turning tons of stone into building blocks. Teams brought equipment and supplies in their suitcases—even a large jackhammer! Team members erected buildings, provided a well, made fence posts, and enclosed 20 acres of the campus. Appropriately, the chapel was the first building erected. Started by four teams from Pasadena, California, First Church, it was finished by several others.

Work and Witness remains one of the major forces in the plans for the university. They have constructed six dormitories, a gazebo, the three-story Grace Roles Library, and five homes for faculty and staff. At the time of this writing another 30 teams, most from the Southeast Region of the United States, have committed to build the 36,000-square-foot, multipurpose Harmon Schmelzenbach Hall and additional dormitory and staff housing. The spiritual impact of these dedicated people has brought salvation and blessing to many throughout Africa.

Grace Roles Library building

Work and Witness blessings are of many kinds. One team in September 1998 included several doctors, who made their services available to the community around the university. They were given permission by health authorities to offer a one-day clinic on the campus. The response was overwhelming. Plans had been made to care for 200 patients in the tiny clinic. At dawn people began to arrive. Before the day was over, more than 1,200 people had come to the campus.

Donors

Mark Moore threw himself into promotion of the university in his deputation services before coming to Africa. Within two years, individuals, churches, districts, companies, and friends had donated more than $1 million in cash as well as hundreds of thousands of dollars of equipment and supplies.

ANU has established an "honors court" at the heart of the campus to recognize donors. Also, volunteers have planted indigenous trees with attached tags that indicate the donors who have contributed to the landscaping. Shrubs and cacti have been set out around the dormitories, and grass and gardens have been planted.

ANU campus

Volunteers

The Lord helped Mark Moore to put together a remarkable support team. At the core were the Helstroms, the Garvins, and the Conrads. They organized teams, bought equipment, gathered books, and filled and shipped containers. Tens of thousands of dollars were saved. Volunteers packed and sent an entire hospital kitchen, valued at $200,000, to ANU. Volunteers secured and furnished six apartments. The bonding between teams, NIVS, missionaries, and nationals grew and gave the feeling that all were working on a God-given mission.

Not all of the volunteers were involved in finance, buildings, and shipping. Many came to teach. When the university was still years away, a diploma program was needed to build on the Intensives and the extension classes. Clarice Moore, in consultation with Professor Lloyd Lunsford and Ted Esselstyn, set up a curriculum for a diploma in theology. Kenya Nazarene Bible College was opened temporarily on the campus of the proposed university. Mark Moore served as principal, and available missionary personnel, such as the Newtons, Joneses, Schmelzenbachs, and Gastineaus, helped with the teaching.

The 12 students enrolled at the start quickly grew to 48 on campus and 170 by extension. Additional teachers were needed, and God supplied them. These valiant volunteers not only gave of themselves and their time but also contributed more than $70,000 for equipment and scholarships and another $100,000 for evangelism. Among them were Raymond Cook, Ray and Lorene Finger, Barrett Kirby, Lloyd Lunsford, Harry and Lora Gilbert, William Fisher, Nellie Montaigne, Pat Westmoreland, Jessie Miller, Lee Jernigan, Esther Lunsford, Connie Cook, and Vic and Darlene Shorb.

CHAPTER 7

OPENING THE UNIVERSITY

The establishment of ANU brought three "firsts": the first new institution the Commission for Higher Education in Kenya was evaluating, the first Nazarene institution to come into existence after the establishment of the International Board of Education (IBOE), and the first Nazarene liberal arts institution outside the United States. Furthermore, both the Kenya commission and the IBOE were new.

The Commission for Higher Education had opened the door for private universities in Kenya. Existing institutions that were affiliated with overseas colleges also needed to meet the requirements of the commission. The proposed Africa Nazarene University was the first new institution under this law, but 27 other institutions were seeking recognition. The commission, though busy, gave generously of its time to assist ANU in preparing the accrediting document. The commission strongly encouraged Dr. Moore to broaden the scope of the intended institution to include nonministerial education. This coincided with the dream from so many years before. At the same time, this presented another complication: the Church of the Nazarene

Manual requires that a liberal arts institution be approved by the General Assembly itself.

The first proposal acquainted the commission with the Church of the Nazarene and its involvement in education around the world. The second document was the start of the official proposal. It took several revisions before the commission granted the Letter of Interim Authority to operate a university in 1994.

Pressure for establishing the university was mounting. The bachelor of theology program offered by Nazarene theological colleges in South Africa and Swaziland was producing a significant group of prospective master's degree students. The church in Kenya had moved to four districts. Demand for university education in Kenya was growing. Some 200,000 Kenyans completed high school yearly, but only 6,000 places were open for those students who wished to continue their education. Kenyan universities turned down 16,000 qualified applicants each year.

Church questions also had to be answered. Was a liberal arts institution advisable for Africa? Was it financially viable? Ted Esselstyn, as a member of IBOE, was able to present the case. The Africa Region committed that the institution would not ask for World Evangelism Fund monies, and that operational costs would be fully covered by tuition. This was a major commitment that some felt could not be done, especially in Africa, the poorest continent. The assistance, guidance, and encouragement received from the IBOE were most helpful.

The IBOE carefully evaluated the constitution of the institution, the control of policy by a Nazarene Board of Trust, the objectives of ANU as a holiness university, and the strategy for financing and staffing the institution. An advisory committee assisted the emerging institution in developing its charter. Finally, in February 1993, the IBOE presented a motion to the General Board for the submission of a resolution to the General Assembly authorizing the establishment of Africa Nazarene University. The Board of General Superintendents and the General Board approved the resolution, and in July the General Assembly unanimously endorsed the proposed university.

Work was continuing at ANU. A key requirement was development of the library. Collections of books came from the libraries of Nazarene scholars, such as Ralph Earle, Seldon Kelly, Willis Lambert, Mark Moore, H. T. Reza, Warren Rood, Charles Strickland, Mildred Bangs Wyncoop, and Samuel Young. A significant collection in the areas of English, reference and religion, purchased by and put together in Ireland under the direction of Ray Cook, is one of the most important acquisitions the library has made. The library now houses some 150,000 volumes. Veteran librarians Richard Schuster and Esther Schandorff gave of their retirement years to direct the library and to sort and catalog the books. Surplus volumes have enriched the libraries of extension programs and the other Nazarene institutions in Africa. The development of the library along with the need for classrooms and of-

ANU's library stacks

fice space necessitated the erection of the Grace Roles Library.

> *"With God's help and to the best of our abilities, we did* what we could, with what we had, where we were."

Dr. Moore's tenure ended in 1991. He had given four years, so vital to the start of ANU. The Moores were not prepared for the farewell scene at the Nairobi airport. Students, faculty, staff, missionaries, and a multitude of friends came to acknowledge the outpouring of the Moores' lives into Kenya. A large sign declared: "Thank you, Dr. and Mrs. Moore. We love you!" Tears and hugs overwhelmed them. Later Mark wrote:

As the plane lifted into the sky, I thought, *What has God wrought these last four years?* Only His leadership could have brought this together—a Bible college, a graduate seminary, and a university; a campus with six buildings, including a chapel at a focal point; adequate water; campus beautification; a host of honorary alumni concerned and praying for ANU. Hundreds have been involved. We thank God for them. Among the number were our two sons. Kent provided an auto for our use. Brad took care of our needs while we were gone and worked with Pat Conrad buying equipment. Suddenly I thought of Laverne Mullen singing at a General Assembly: "Little Is Much When God Is in It." Clarice and I stretched out with pillows under our heads, a blanket over us in the packed tourist cabin section. Memories flooded my mind. This special assignment is over. With God's help and to the best of our abilities, we did *what we could, with what we had, where we were."*

These last three short phrases were the hallmark of Mark Moore. He challenged everyone to do the same with the help of God.

Dr. Al Jones, under the guidance of the Board of General Superintendents, was chosen to carry the task forward. Al and Kitty Jones had served in Kenya, Australia, and the United States. Al did two important things. First, he brought to the university, on a two-year commitment, Dr. Robert and Sue Woodruff with whom he had been acquainted in

Australia. Bob, who had served as interim rector of European Nazarene Bible College in Switzerland, became academic dean. With his knowledge of Commonwealth universities, he was able to structure the academic program of the university to meet the requirements of the Commission for Higher Education. Second, he upgraded the Bible college program and paved the way for the transfer of the Kenya Nazarene Bible College out of the university into the hands of the field.

The building program at the ANU campus was affected by Desert Storm in the Middle East. One Work and Witness team was briefly stranded when U.S. planes were conscripted for troop transport. Word got out that Kenya was near Kuwait, even though it is more than 2,000 miles away. The influx of teams slowed down and the completion of buildings became a major challenge.

Al and Kitty saw two great things happen. The first was the passing of the resolution at the July 1993 General Assembly for the establishment of Africa Nazarene University. This made it official from the church's standpoint. The second was the receipt of the "Letter of Interim Authority" from the Commission for Higher Education in September 1993 that granted permission to open a university. Now it was essential to recruit students and have the campus ready for them by August 1994. At least the first two floors of the library had to be usable, and one dormitory had to be converted into a kitchen and dining room. Later, when Al and Kitty Jones were appointed to take over Nazarene mission work in Ethiopia, another vice-chancellor was needed.

God had prepared. A few weeks earlier Drs. Martha and Floyd John, with major responsibilities in education and in computer technology in Washington, D.C., had written to the then education commissioner, Stephen Neese, indicating they would like to help on an overseas assignment. Dr.

Martha John

Nease contacted Ted Esselstyn who then met with Floyd and Martha. They eagerly accepted the ANU assignment, Martha as vice-chancellor and Floyd as academic dean to replace Bob Woodruff.

These were critical days for the university. The load that descended upon the Johns' hardworking and capable shoulders was enormous. The completion of the library building to also serve as classroom and offices was priority. There was no money to complete the work, and significant deficits existed. Dormitory space would accommodate 65 students, and the break-even point for a tuition-driven institution was 300. Only 65 students would require massive subsidization.

ANU opened in August 1994, offering bachelor degrees in theology and business administration, and a master of arts in religion. What a great day!

The poverty of many Nazarene students tore at the hearts of the faculty and administration. Several refugee students came from Rwanda and Burundi, both countries in the midst of wars. The financial situation was compounded by the reluctance of ANU to insist upon payment of accounts. The Johns and their team made a tremendous effort to meet the financial challenge. They found many donors who helped provide funds. Compassionate Ministries provided scholarships for refugee and underprivileged students. The Africa Region gave heavily from its resources. The combination kept the institution functioning. The financial pressures of paying off the library building and meeting the daily expenses were overwhelming.

Security became a problem. Bandits thought the university, somewhat isolated from the city, would be an easy target. Martha John had to upgrade security, which was costly. When a door opened for the purchase of 10 acres, Dr. John purchased the land with the support of Bob and

Yvonne Helstrom. This paved the way for the purchase of an additional 20 with the right-of-way for a new road. The successful completion of the first year of operation was a triumph. The relationship between students and teaching staff was high. There was great excitement for the new year.

Floyd John is a computer expert. He learned there was little opportunity in Nairobi for anyone to secure good computer training. Only one university offered a degree in computer science and accepted just a handful of top students each year. When ANU considered a bachelor's degree in computer science, the Commission for Higher Education was excited. Plans were made to take in the first class in August 1995. Applications poured in. Only one of every 50 applicants could be accepted. Everything looked good. The major difficulty was finance for students wanting to enter the Th.B. program in preparation for the ministry.

In African society, the larger family, including aunts, uncles, and cousins, often join together to support a person admitted to a university. Sometimes a whole village or chieftainship will unite to support an outstanding student. Only in this way can students meet the costs. Tuition, board, and room amounted to $3,000 for one year at ANU. By American standards this is cheap, far less than America's gross national product (GNP) of $25,000 per person. But by African standards, it is astronomical. Students from 13 nations of Africa attended ANU in 1995. Of these 13 countries the nation with the highest GNP per capita was Swaziland with $1,170. Mozambique had the lowest GNP per capita with an incredibly low $80. Most of the African countries represented, such as Kenya, had a GNP per capita around $300. This means that 1 year at ANU would cost an American less than 2 months earnings. Yet a Kenyan would pay 10 years of earnings and a Mozambican 37 years and 6 months of earnings. Scholarships are imperative, especially for ministers. There is no way that a student can earn enough in the African economy to pay for a university education.

During the second year, the financial stress became intolerable. Martha and Floyd John gave of themselves beyond the call of duty. Finally, health concerns compelled them to return to the United States. They had made vital contributions at incredible personal expense. With sadness the university community saw their departure and scrambled to find administrative and computer staff as well as finances to keep the university open. But God's Word is true. The Lord is "an ever-present help in trouble" (Psalm 46:1). The university stayed open.

Missionary faculty members, Jim and Carol Rotz, stepped into the gap and added to their teaching load the responsibility for administration and academics. Without their competence and sacrificial work, the university would have closed. Visiting teachers, such as John and Pat Thomas, went the second mile to keep students on schedule. Ted and Joan Esselstyn broke free of other responsibilities and spent months at ANU to help out. The Board of Trust elected Ted as chancellor and charged him with the search for a new vice-chancellor.

Dr. Leah Marangu became the first Kenyan woman to hold the position of vice-chancellor of a university.

John and Leah Marangu had just returned to Kenya. They had been teaching in the United States, he at Olivet Nazarene University and Point Loma Nazarene University, and she establishing a department of Christian home in a state university. Professor Leah Marangu was, and still is, a member of the Commission for Higher Education. When Chancellor Esselstyn met John and Leah Marangu officially, he asked Leah if she would consider taking the responsibility of vice-chancellor. She responded that she felt God had been preparing her for that very task.

At the January 1996 meeting of the Board of Trust, Leah Marangu was unanimously elected vice-chancellor of Africa Nazarene University. She became the first Kenyan woman to hold the position of vice-chancellor of a university.

The first challenge the new vice-chancellor faced was additional staff. Bob Bollinger, retired vice president for finance at Eastern Nazarene College, came to ANU with his wife, Lucy, to set up the financial system. Accounting policies were put into effect and a loan worked out to get the university through the remainder of the year. Mike and Renee

Servis, she a certified public accountant from Utah, offered their services to World Mission and agreed to come to ANU. This was a double blessing, for Mike, who had owned a computer network servicing company, provided the university with needed computer expertise.

Dr. Marangu found qualified, experienced Kenyan administrators. Timothy Kihiko came to the registrar's office, and Paul Kang'ori became dean of students and services. Both acted as if 20-hour workdays were the norm. They became the backbone in developing the administration. Everyone worked overtime, and the second year closed successfully with the university solvent.

In the third year, when the enrollment jumped to 260, additional teachers were needed. The Rotzes were leaving on furlough, and even the religion department was short-staffed. Gary and Janice Goodell, he the dean of Swaziland Nazarene Bible College, and Thomas and Ethel Lowry, he the principal of Nazarene Theological College of Central Africa in Malawi, agreed to move to ANU. Local nationals and missionaries filled in the gaps.

The third year proved to be a busy one. Since the Commission for Higher Education planned its next visit during the fourth year, everything needed to be ready and in place. Curriculum committees were put to work. Buildings were brought up to standard. The top floor of the library had to be completed. Another dormitory was needed.

Travel to the campus by day students and staff is a problem because of the distance from the main road and the road's poor condition. University buses help, but during the rainy season life can be difficult. Much of the soil is "black cotton" that becomes miry when wet. Sometimes even the 4x4s get stuck, and walking is the only way in. Over and over the Marangus' personal sedan was disabled by the horrible shape of the road. Leah convinced local authorities to upgrade the road, but heavy trucks and every rain shower defeated all efforts. When the university was able to secure a suitable four-wheel drive for the vice-chancellor's use, everyone rejoiced.

Students lived in overcrowded dormitories, frequently six in a room designed for four. Yet the spirit among the students was excellent; these "pio-

ANU chapel, the first building erected by
Work and Witness teams.

neers" were determined to earn a good education. Chapel was well attended, but the students and staff comfortably filled the structure. The dream had been too small. The planners had thought of a seminary when the chapel was built, and the 400-seat capacity had seemed generous. But special events could not be held in the chapel. The installation service for Vice-Chancellor Marangu with more than a thousand attending had to be held outdoors. The front-page-news event was followed by a special education insert in the leading Saturday paper. This publicity resulted in more applications, and enrollment for the fourth year topped 400. Plans had to be made to expand the chapel.

The dreams had been more than fulfilled.

CHAPTER 8

LOOKING AT STUDENT LIFE

Spiritual life at ANU is strong. Students organized "Morning Glory," a devotional group that meets before breakfast, as well as other prayer groups.

Africans love to sing. The student-directed choir of 40 members has participated in city events, such as the production of "The Messiah." The choir is well known for their Zulu song, "Jabulani Africa" (Rejoice Africa). Student composers write songs and music. Singing groups abound.

ANU choir

Campus life includes the work-study program during the school year and a work program especially for foreign students during the holidays. This enables some students to earn some money toward their expenses.

Students enjoy many activities and sports available on campus—soccer, volleyball, basketball, chess, draughts (checkers), Scrabble, and darts. Also they enjoy the tours, arranged from time to time, to game reserves and other areas of Africa. Holiday tours to distant countries enhance learning and promote the exchange of ideas with young people in other parts of the continent.

* * *

During the past few years, many students have written letters to ANU. Here is how a few have described their university experience.

Effient Masoamphambe, a business student from Malawi, loves to write. He tends to be somewhat philosophical.

Africa Nazarene University has a mission to train future Christian leaders for Africa. Our continent is well known for poverty, disease, war, corruption, and political instability. These problems can be solved by leaders who have Christian values, have been well trained academically, and have social skills. The best place to prepare such leaders is ANU. Being a student at ANU is a big step in the process of transformation. The organization of knowledge through lectures and interaction with other students changes one's way of thinking, worldview, and behavior.

After four years at ANU, I expect to have the ability to face life with a positive attitude. ANU students come from different countries around Africa. After graduation, each one will go back home and apply what has been learned. This will bring a change in society. It is difficult to know which students are enrolled in computer science, business administration, theology, or the preparatory program. Most visitors think we are all taking theology because of the spiritual atmosphere on the campus.

ANU strives to make us complete persons —spiritually, academically, and socially. ANU believes that it is the combination of these elements that makes a true leader. The primary problem of our world is spiritual. If this is properly cared for, in context, then other needed changes will follow. It is hoped eventually the ANU's products—the students—will not only make a difference in their home countries but also will come back to teach and assist in making the university truly African. This will complete the circle of obedience to the commands of Jesus Christ to live out His life in this world.

"Education without Christ is absolutely incomplete and is like a river without a source."

Last year Effient wrote a remarkable letter, stating he had discovered he could do a lot with his acquired knowledge to help his home church in Malawi. Most Christians there are subsistence farmers who grow crops to feed their families but are often hit by food shortages common in most African countries.

I know that Malawi has enough resources for self-support. I am now one of the people who can help develop those skills and potential-ities through basic education and training so that we can face the challenges of self-support boldly and courageously. Include me in your secret prayer. Education without Christ is absolutely incomplete and is like a river without a source.

Fastone Sabwera, another Malawian, is the child of one of our first pastors.

As a pastor's son, I'm proud and thrilled about the development that has taken place in this institution. This is really a sacrifice the church has made. I just see the glory of the Lord. I am one of the students who has been privileged to work to raise my fees. The work has given me practical experience in the world of work. The happiest time of my life is when I am singing in the Shalom quartet. The saddest time is when a student has to go home because he or she cannot pay school fees. Any amount sent to the university in the form of a grant or scholarship, no matter how little, is a blessing to needy students.

Aurelia Mutesa, a young woman from Zambia, is enrolled in the business course.

I received the Lord as my Savior in 1987, and since that time He has been my Shepherd. I thank God for giving me the opportunity to come to ANU. It is not that I am better than others are, but I believe the Lord has a purpose for me. ANU is a wonderful campus because Christian discipline is effected everywhere. I have never regretted being here. I believe that by the time students graduate they will be good role models wherever they go.

Andrew Chikazi from Zimbabwe is one of the many computer science students.

I was born again when I was 17 years old, and I thank God for the great transformation that happened in my life. Being away from

ANU students taking exams

home has not changed my commitment to God, but instead it has helped me realize that I can also be faithful to God without my parents' reminders. After graduation my plans are to go into business. I believe that God can use laypeople as well as ministers to work in His kingdom. I want to use the knowledge I acquire as a tool to reach out to people. If the Satanists and other cultists are able to show their evil ideas to people on the Net, why shouldn't we Christians use it also?

Emmanuel Epedu from Uganda is enrolled in the business administration program.

I was born and brought up in a Christian family. My parents have been active in God's ministry. I have seen how good God has been to them. He has been good to me. I intend to do something for Him. I felt that God's will for me was business administration. I have no intention of becoming an employee. I want to be a risk-taker. ANU is a nice place. What I like most is the Christian morals ANU tries to maintain. It holds chapels and a service on Sunday. In addition, the students have organized Bible studies, prayer meetings, fellowships, and morning devotions. What I have gained from these meetings cannot be obtained in a non-Christian university. We are being trained to become leaders with a difference, leaders with knowledge and Christian morals.

Monica Amiji, also a business administration major from Uganda, has gone through difficult times since coming to ANU.

"I thank God for the spirit of oneness in this university."

I am now an orphan. My mum died when I was young, and my dad died last year. Though I have had a lot of hardships, I praise my Lord because when I am broken down He lifts me up; when I am about to lose hope, He strengthens me. I cannot forget the time I lost my father. I thought his death had destroyed any hope for my future. The staff, students, and especially the vice-chancellor, who acted like my mother to comfort me even though she had a very busy schedule, joined together to give me hope and make it possible for me to continue my studies. I thank God for the spirit of oneness in this university. I have no words to express my gratitude, and I continue praying for ANU and the missionaries. My future plan is to help orphans and use what God has given me to build His kingdom and for His glory.

Aboma Bayessa, an Ethiopian in the bachelor of theology program, became a Christian in 1986 in western Ethiopia.

I had fled my home area to Addis Ababa because of persecution. At one time, I was put in jail because I refused to renounce my Christian testimony. A Christian friend gave me opportunity to come to Kenya to continue my studies. I joined a university but soon realized that it was not for me. God wanted me for His ministry. I then joined ANU. Since coming here I received bad news. My brother died in an Ethiopian plane crash in the Comoros Islands [the same crash that took the life of missionary Ron Farris]. At the same time, my sponsor stopped helping me. It is a miracle that I am still here. I am thankful for the ANU scholarship I have received. It made possible my plan to continue my studies and then go back home to serve the Lord.

* * *

The students who have the greatest difficulty at ANU are those who come from the Portuguese- and French-speaking countries of Africa. They completed their high school studies, not in English, but in Portuguese or French, and merely took English as a subject. Nevertheless, many students have come to ANU from these countries.

Lote Jonas Mulate is the son of a former Nazarene district superintendent in Mozambique and now a missionary in Angola. Both his grandfathers were Nazarene district superintendents.

I have been involved in church activities since the age of 12. This did not make me a Christian. I accepted Jesus as my personal Savior, and He made me His son and a sheep of

His flock. Mozambique is a country that was ravaged by war for more than 20 years. God has restored peace. To have a higher education was one of my great desires. With the situation in my country, it seemed impossible. When I read of ANU in the *Trans African* magazine, it brought excitement, but I did not think I could make it. I applied, and the response was positive. The next problem was to pay my fees. I remembered that God is the owner of all riches, all silver and gold belong to Him. I prayed, and He answered my prayer. God inspired someone to give, and I was awarded a scholarship for the year. I would like to commend the work of Professor Marangu and her staff to make ANU a better place.

Sophie Bugenimana, a business administration major, is Rwandese. Her husband is completing his master's degree at ANU. Both are refugees, and though Sophie struggled to learn English, she became a top student.

I am married and have nine children. I am saved, washed in the blood of the Lamb. Born in a strong and fervent Catholic family, I found myself without hope and peace. I tried to do good works and wrote personal verses to please the Lord, but still a vacuum was in my heart. In 1977 I heard about Jesus' love and power to forgive. I repented, my burden was taken away, and my heart was filled with joy. I came to Kenya because of the great tribulation that shook my country, Rwanda. God was with us on our long journey. ANU authorities sympathized with me and not only admitted us but gave me a job in the registrar's office. Both my husband and I worked hard on campus during holidays to pay tuition fees. I love ANU for the way it stands as a Christian institution and because the authorities care for the students. I want to finish my studies and go on for a Ph.D. Marketers can be job creators, and my country needs job creators. When things settle down, I will return to Rwanda where I hope to be useful in rebuilding my country.

Suy-Bi Goore Fortune is the first student at ANU from the West African country of Côte d'Ivoire. Even though his studies were previously in French, he excels in academics.

While in secondary school, I used to look down on Christians and thought they were wasting their time on nonsense called Christianity. I was attracted to spiritism and oriental religions. I used to trust in my intelligence to succeed in life. When I got sick and was obliged to leave school, I saw all my dreams collapse. I was in a distressful life of pain, rejection, and loneliness. I gave careful thought to Christianity. My father passed away. I was hopeless and empty. Then one day I got the right message, 'We have a common enemy, the devil, but Jesus came to set us free. You should not leave this place today, brother, without

ANU dormitories

making peace with your God and your Lord.' I
gave my life to Jesus. God showed me other
burdened souls and His desire for me to serve
Him. I completed the diploma in Bible studies
at the Nazarene college in Abidjan. I felt deep-
er studies would benefit my service to the
Lord, and He opened the door for me to go to
ANU where I am in the theology program. I
praise God for the opportunity to be here. I feel
companionship with my brothers and sisters.
God bless those who made it possible for me to
be here.

Bukuru Sebastien is from Burundi where civil
war is still intermittently going on. He grew up in a
Christian home and worked four years as a teacher

in a secondary school before God called him into the ministry.

Many people asked why I had decided to change my career. I told them that it was not for me to decide, it was God who had called me. When I arrived in Nairobi, I heard of ANU and applied. I found a nice, peaceful place for studies. Above all, I felt I was in a family because of the spirit of unity and cooperation between students and administration. Everyone is concerned about each other. Even in times of problems, no one can feel alone. Last year one brother and one sister were killed. The ANU family comforted me, especially Vice-Chancellor Leah Marangu. I want to go back to my country as a preacher and teacher of God's word.

Atsidri Assia, from the Democratic Republic of the Congo, is in the business course. He was sent to Kenya by a supporter to attend ANU.

"My experience at ANU has made my faith grow."

Two weeks before I joined ANU, my financial supporter was no more. I came to school anyway, trusting God to do something. Two days before the opening, I got a message to meet someone downtown in Nairobi. A miracle happened. I was given a check as a gift to pay my fees. I could not believe my eyes. The Lord had met my need at the last minute. My experience at ANU has made my faith grow. I trust God for my needs. ANU has the vision to train leaders for Africa. The continent needs such leaders. The academic, spiritual, and social development I am getting here is preparing me to face the challenges of life. Last year when war broke out again in eastern Democratic Republic of Congo, the area where my family lives was under rebel control. I was shocked and saddened to hear that friends were killed. I would appreciate your prayers for peace in my country.

* * *

The great majority of the students at ANU are from Kenya. This is natural because of ANU's location along with the publicity it receives. It is also the area of east Africa where the Church of the Nazarene is strongest. From the many students from Kenya who have written, here are a few of their comments.

Edwin Wanyonyi, a business administration major, is an Anglican and attended mission schools. He came to ANU because of the excellence of the program and the fact that computer studies were required of all students.

At ANU there is spiritual nourishment. Under the guidance of Chaplain Goodell and Dr. Lowry, we students receive great blessings. Chapel is an encouragement to many students to give their lives to the Lord. The choir has become a tool for evangelism. To keep fit we enjoy the games on campus, including football, volleyball, softball, and basketball. The vice-chancellor and others have accomplished much, but there are drawbacks. There are not enough buildings for the increasing number of students. More up-to-date equipment is needed to maintain the quality of the programs. Despite this, ANU is a place where Christian morals and virtues are taught and modeled. Special thanks to the Church of the Nazarene.

Jacqueline Odero is in the business administration program. She, too, is a Nazarene who grew up in Sunday School and participated in church choirs and youth groups. Her father was one of the first district superintendents in northwest Kenya. She accepted Christ as her personal Savior while in high school.

> *"I like ANU because it molds people to be more upright in society as Christians and leaders."*

This experience changed my life completely. I chose to live for God. It is my joy that I am forgiven of my sins and called into the family of God. God has carried me through very painful and bitter experiences in life. My father died while I was in high school. My mother died last year. As the first born of a family of five, I became responsible for my younger brothers and sisters. At the beginning, I did not know how I would manage or cope with this situation. I felt that God had allowed a very big loss in our lives. But God stood by me and has carried me through. The most remarkable thing in my life is that God owns all of my times—times of happiness and sorrow, my time now, and best of all, my future. My father had told me of ANU while I was in high school, while ANU was still in the planning. He promised to bring me to ANU when I finished high school. He died in my final year, but through God's miracle I was able to come. I love it here. It is a very beautiful place with wonderful people. I have had really wide exposure and have met people from different cultures and backgrounds. Above all, I like ANU because it molds people to be more upright in society as Christians and leaders.

Henry Akendo is studying for the ministry. He grew up in a polygamous home, the sixth of seven children. He was saved in 1982.

When I first learned of ANU, I knew that this was the place for me. The university is out of town, a quiet environment for study. The scenery is beautiful, including the game animals. Anyone who comes to ANU feels at home. I am captain of the volleyball team and a member of the soccer team. Life is exciting. My only problem is meeting the costs, but God enables us to complete that which He starts in us.

Samuel Kariuki was superintendent of the Kenya Northeast District of the Church of the Nazarene.

My father was a witch doctor, well known, feared, and respected. He was used to evil spirits and did wonders that amazed people. Those who needed healing or to appease evil spirits came to him and received the desires of their hearts. My mother also performed the same dirty things. There are nine children in our family. We were brought up with all sorts of wickedness. We did not know church or the Word of God. We lived in a world of our own, an island of witchcraft and traditional beliefs. We had no hope, living under fear and the tortures of evil spirits.

At the age of 20, I heard Jesus preached for the first time. I listened, though it didn't make sense to me in the beginning. As the message continued, I sensed the need to accept Christ. When the altar call was made, I went forward and committed my life to Christ. I repented and Christ forgave me. I felt joy, hope, and assurance. Jesus Christ removed all fear and gave me a divine peace. My parents kicked me out of the family. They cursed me and told me to go away with my foreign gods. Foreign gods (Christianity) had nothing to do with their gods (traditional beliefs, ancestors). I experienced a lonely life, but I had the Lord.

My prayer was that God should visit our family in a miraculous way. God heard, and in

Rev. Samuel Kariuki

1972 my mother was saved. It was great and encouraging, and it caused joy and curiosity. In the same year my younger brother was saved. Miraculously, God's divine intervention restored me to my family. Although my father continued to torture us, God continued to do great things. Finally, in 1987, God did a remarkable miracle, and this famous witch doctor found Jesus Christ as his personal Savior. He was filled with the Holy Spirit and sanctified. Today we are all Nazarenes, washed by the blood, filled by the Spirit.

I started feeling that God wanted me to do something for Him. I made up my mind to obey, went to Bible College, graduated, and then went to Great Britain to take a course in missiology. I was introduced to the Church of the Nazarene by Rev. G. K. Adams, a pastor in Northern Ireland. On returning to Kenya, I found the church and joined. I worked with the church for 10 years. During that time I was elected district superintendent. In 1994 I resigned as district superintendent to enter ANU. Coming here was a dream come true. May God bless those who have helped me.

Samuel Kariuki is now superintendent of the Kenya Central District. Julius Njuki, his predecessor, resigned to start his studies for the Th.B. at ANU.

Rev. Tekle G. Mariam, first
graduate from Ethiopia.

Rev. Wellington Obotte,
Nazarene missionary
to Tanzania.

Christine Tindi,
covaledictorian of first
graduation class.

Carlos Mbanze, first
graduate from
Mozambique.

CHAPTER 9

GRANTING DEGREES

Saturday, May 23, 1998, dawned brightly on ANU's campus. Glorious sunshine followed days of rain. Nine great white canopies stretched out in the university square. Thousands of flowers formed exquisite arrangements on the supporting poles before the platform. From early morning vehicles bustled back and forth from hotels and churches, bringing in the folks. Cars, trucks, and buses crowded onto the fields about the campus. People flocked to tents seeking their chairs. Ushers worked hard to get everyone to the appropriate sections, carefully guarding the reserved seats. Prominent guests, university officials, and state dignitaries moved to the VIP section. Many church leaders from districts, fields, and the whole Africa Region found their places. Choirs and students were prepared. With microphones tested and various instruments tuned, everything was ready.

And then it began—the first graduation at Africa Nazarene University, the fulfillment of a dream. These graduates were the first fruits of faith. The choir stood and began to sing. With the banner raised high, the procession flowed from the door of the library past the chapel and clock tower to the platform. First came the 25 graduating students who would receive their bachelor's or master's de-

Graduation procession, l. to r.: Ted Esselstyn,
Leah Marangu, Mark Moore, John Bowling.

grees. Then came the teaching staff, trust members, honored guests, and, at the rear, the chancellor and vice-chancellor. The robes were of many colors— black and red and blue, yellow and green—with stoles and hoods, with gold braid and tassels, and a variety of caps—all the trimmings of academia.

As the procession drew to an end, Rev. David Holmes, former pastor of the first Nazarene Church in Kenya, Nairobi Central, and current district superintendent of the KwaZulu Natal District in South Africa, prayed the invocation. Chancellor Theodore Esselstyn convened the congregation, and the convocation was under way.

Two hymns had been specially chosen, "To God Be the Glory" at the start and "Guide Me, O Thou Great Jehovah" at the close. The ANU choir, the Shalom quartet, and Point Loma Nazarene University students provided uplifting music. And a choir of colorful Masai women from the community joined their traditional song of blessing to the exuberance of the day.

Vice-Chancellor Leah Marangu extended a welcome to all, presented her vision for the future of the university, and expressed her joy at the students' success in reaching this goal. Her challenge was to excellence and integrity in every walk of life. She praised the two women who stood at the top of the class—one, a bright young girl, and the other, a mother of nine. Then the degrees were granted. It culminated with the granting of an honorary doctor of letters to Mark Reynolds Moore, the godly man responsible for the groundwork in establishing the university.

The tables, flowers, decor,
and food all shouted out,
"Celebration! Praise be to God!"

Dr. John Bowling, president of Olivet Nazarene University (ONU), was the honored speaker. His message, "The Magnificent Obsession," challenged all. With him were his chief administrators, also representing this great institution. The support of ONU had been and still is vital in the establishment and continued operation of ANU.

Four professors representing Point Loma Nazarene University (PLNU) were in the procession. They had brought a contingent of PLNU stu-

Mark Moore being awarded Doctor of Letters
at first graduation.

First graduation class in 1998

dents to the campus for external studies, and the students became a part of the music activities. One of these professors, David Whitelaw, prayed the benediction.

At the conclusion of the ceremony came the feast. The tables, flowers, decor, and food all shouted out, "Celebration! Praise be to God!"

＊　＊　＊

All of the gracious and glowing words of the leaders, the visitors, and the students were fine, but then the true test came. ANU faculty and staff wondered if the graduates were truly prepared to make a difference in "the real world." The university and church leaders believed they were.

Yet, there was still so much to do to make Africa Nazarene University the beacon that Christ wants it to be: classes to be continued, programs to be devised, buildings to be constructed, staff to be recruited.

ANU's fourth year was a time of triumph and challenge. The Commission for Higher Education had been pleased with the progress and with the future plans. The faculty and staff were encouraged and thus challenged to continue developing the university.

In January 1998, when the trust met to plan for the first graduation, the first joy was the report of the auditors, Deloitte and Touche. After the auditors examined the books, they were pleased with the accounting. The university was solvent, and the hope of being tuition-driven was a reality, for student tuition was able to cover operation costs once enrollment exceeded 200 students.

Harmon Schmelzenbach Hall under construction

The second joy was that the next major building project, the Harmon Schmelzenbach Hall, could be started. This large, four-floor structure, when finished, will provide dining facilities, classrooms, dormitory space, and offices. The project was undertaken largely by the churches and districts of the Southeast U.S.A. Region under the leadership of Dennis Moore, general NWMS council member. The region committed to sending more than a score of Work and Witness teams. At the same time, a block of senior staff housing is also under construction with the help of other Work and Witness teams.

Additional staff members have joined the university. Henry Kiongo has come to be the estate manager, and his expertise has greatly improved the appearance of the campus. Others have arrived to assist with administration, bringing many talents to bear upon the many challenges. A development office has been established to promote the needs of the university among the many organizations that assist with education worldwide.

But ANU's faculty and staff must never forget that their task is primarily a spiritual one. Effient Masoamphambe, in his letter, wrote: "Education without Christ is like a river without a source." This is true. The university's objective is to ground every student in Christ, that they might know, love, and serve Him. This is one thing that the enemy would fight. And fight he does! Forces are at work that would overthrow Christian principles. Sometimes, the evil one is able to find an avenue to stir up students or parents or anyone to destroy the work of Christ.

The faculty and staff request that Nazarenes intercede for Africa Nazarene University. The school's function is to provide holiness higher education for the youth of Africa, so that they will go forth well prepared to live and proclaim the fullness of the gospel before all people. Pray for "the Lord of the harvest to send out laborers . . ." (Matthew 9:38, RSV).

There is no desire on the part of the trust, the administration, or the staff to simply have an educational institution. ANU wants to provide the best in education and stimulate the students to holy living. The university's theme is "excellence in education." But this is only possible when people are grounded in the river of life that flows through Jesus Christ and His Holy Spirit.

What does the future hold? God knows. ANU's faculty and staff seek His direction in every expansion of curriculum and student body. Will there be agriculture, mathematics, science, and history departments? Will there be an extension system with branch campuses all over Africa linked together via the Internet or satellite? Will there be a thousand students or perhaps even more?

These are all a part of the hopes and dreams. Yet, the people at ANU have vividly seen how God plans. He turns *dreams* into *open doors* and *degrees*—through His people.

PRONUNCIATION GUIDE

The following information is provided to assist in pronouncing unfamiliar words in the book. The suggested pronunciations, though not always precise, are close approximations of the way the terms are pronounced in English.

Aboma Bayessa	ah-BOHM-ah bah-YEH-sah
Akendo	ah-KEHN-doh
Amiji	ah-MEE-djee
Atsidri Assia	aht-SEE-dree ah-SEE-ah
Bugenimana	boo-geh-nee-MAH-nah
Bukuru Sebastien	boo-KOO-roo seh-BAHS-tee-ehn
Chikazi	chih-KAH-zee
Effient Masoamphambe	EHF-ee-ehnt mah-soh-ahm-PAHM-beh
Epedu	eh-PEH-doo
Esselstyn	EHS-uhl-stuhn
Fastone Sabwera	FAH-stohn sah-BWEH-rah
Gastineau	GAS-tuh-noh
harambee	hah-RAHM-bee
Harare	huh-RAH-reh
Horison	hoh-RIEZ-uhn
Jabulani	djah-boo-LAH-nee
Kang'ori	kang-GOH-ree
Kariuki	kah-ree-YOO-kee
Kehm	KEHM
Kenyatta	kehn-YAH-tah
Kihikho	kih-HEE-koh

Kimbui	kim-BOO-ee
Kiongo	kee-AHN-goh
Litswele	liht-SWEH-leh
Lodrich Gama	LOH-drihk GAH-mah
Lote Mulate	LOH-teh moo-LAH-teh
Masai	MAH-sie
Malawi	muh-LAH-wee
Marangu	mah-RAHN-goo
matatus	mah-TAH-toos
Mkabela	mm-kah-BEH-lah
Mokwena	moh-KWEH-nah
Mpoke	mm-POH-keh
Mungai	moon-GIE
Mutesa	moo-TEH-sah
Muthuri	moo-TOO-ree
Ndzimandze	nn-dzee-MAHN-zee
Njuki	nn-DJOO-kee
Odero	oh-DEH-roh
Roodepoort	ROO-deh-poort
Schmelzenbach	SHMEHL-zehn-bah
Sekhukhuneland	seh-koo-KOO-nuh-land
Siteki	sih-TEH-kee
Suy-Bi Goore	soo-bee-GOO-ray
Wanyonyi	wahn-YOWN-ee
Zimbabwe	zihm-BAHB-weh